Productivity Planner

FOR FREELANCE WRITERS

KICKSTART YOUR FREELANCE WRITING CAREER WITH A
FREE 7-DAY EMAIL COURSE AT:
HTTPS://MAMAHUSTLEREPEAT.COM/KICKSTART-
WRITING-CAREER

ALREADY AN EXPERIENCED WRITER? CHECK OUT
MAMAHUSTLEREPEAT.COM FOR MORE FREE
RESOURCES.

Quarterly Goals

SET YOUR PUBLISHING, INCOME, AND CLIENT GOALS
FOR THE NEXT 90 DAYS.

Quarterly Goals

THIS QUARTER'S FOCUS: _____

NOTES:

GOAL 1: _____
ACTION STEPS + DUE DATES:

- _____
- _____
- _____
- _____

GOAL 2: _____
ACTION STEPS + DUE DATES:

- _____
- _____
- _____
- _____

GOAL 3: _____
ACTION STEPS + DUE DATES:

- _____
- _____
- _____
- _____

GOAL 4: _____
ACTION STEPS + DUE DATES:

- _____
- _____
- _____
- _____

Quarterly Goals

DATE RANGE:

THIS QUARTER'S FOCUS: _____

NOTES:

GOAL 1: _____
ACTION STEPS + DUE DATES:
-
-
-
-

GOAL 2: _____
ACTION STEPS + DUE DATES:
-
-
-
-

GOAL 3: _____
ACTION STEPS + DUE DATES:
-
-
-
-

GOAL 4: _____
ACTION STEPS + DUE DATES:
-
-
-
-

Quarterly Goals

THIS QUARTER'S FOCUS: _____

NOTES:

GOAL 1: _____
ACTION STEPS + DUE DATES:

- [ ] _____
- [ ] _____
- [ ] _____
- [ ] _____

GOAL 2: _____
ACTION STEPS + DUE DATES:

- [ ] _____
- [ ] _____
- [ ] _____
- [ ] _____

GOAL 3: _____
ACTION STEPS + DUE DATES:

- [ ] _____
- [ ] _____
- [ ] _____
- [ ] _____

GOAL 4: _____
ACTION STEPS + DUE DATES:

- [ ] _____
- [ ] _____
- [ ] _____
- [ ] _____

Quarterly Goals

THIS QUARTER'S FOCUS: _____

GOAL 1: _____
ACTION STEPS + DUE DATES:

- _____
- _____
- _____
- _____

GOAL 2: _____
ACTION STEPS + DUE DATES:

- _____
- _____
- _____
- _____

GOAL 3: _____
ACTION STEPS + DUE DATES:

- _____
- _____
- _____
- _____

GOAL 4: _____
ACTION STEPS + DUE DATES:

- _____
- _____
- _____
- _____

NOTES:

Client Profiles

KEEP TRACK OF INDIVIDUAL CLIENT'S CONTENT GOALS,
STYLE GUIDELINES, AND IDEAS.

Client Profile

Client:

MONTH FOCUS

STYLE GUIDE

ASSIGNMENTS DUE

ARTICLE IDEAS TO PITCH

OTHER INFO

RATE & FREQUENCY

Client Profile

Client:

MONTH FOCUS

STYLE GUIDE

ASSIGNMENTS DUE

ARTICLE IDEAS TO PITCH

OTHER INFO

RATE & FREQUENCY

Client Profile

Client:

MONTH FOCUS

STYLE GUIDE

ASSIGNMENTS DUE

ARTICLE IDEAS TO PITCH

OTHER INFO

RATE & FREQUENCY

Client Profile

MONTH FOCUS

STYLE GUIDE

ASSIGNMENTS DUE

ARTICLE IDEAS TO PITCH

OTHER INFO

RATE & FREQUENCY

Client Profile

Client:

MONTH FOCUS

STYLE GUIDE

ASSIGNMENTS DUE

ARTICLE IDEAS TO PITCH

OTHER INFO

RATE & FREQUENCY

Client Profile

Client:

MONTH FOCUS

STYLE GUIDE

ASSIGNMENTS DUE

ARTICLE IDEAS TO PITCH

OTHER INFO

RATE & FREQUENCY

Client Profile

Client:

MONTH FOCUS

STYLE GUIDE

ASSIGNMENTS DUE

ARTICLE IDEAS TO PITCH

OTHER INFO

RATE & FREQUENCY

Client Profile

Client:

MONTH FOCUS

STYLE GUIDE

ASSIGNMENTS DUE

ARTICLE IDEAS TO PITCH

OTHER INFO

RATE & FREQUENCY

Client Profile

Client:

MONTH FOCUS

STYLE GUIDE

ASSIGNMENTS DUE

ARTICLE IDEAS TO PITCH

OTHER INFO

RATE & FREQUENCY

Client Profile

Client:

MONTH FOCUS

STYLE GUIDE

ASSIGNMENTS DUE

ARTICLE IDEAS TO PITCH

OTHER INFO

RATE & FREQUENCY

Client Profile

Client:

MONTH FOCUS

STYLE GUIDE

ASSIGNMENTS DUE

ARTICLE IDEAS TO PITCH

OTHER INFO

RATE & FREQUENCY

Client Profile

Client:

MONTH FOCUS

STYLE GUIDE

ASSIGNMENTS DUE

ARTICLE IDEAS TO PITCH

OTHER INFO

RATE & FREQUENCY

Client Profile

Client:

MONTH FOCUS

STYLE GUIDE

ASSIGNMENTS DUE

ARTICLE IDEAS TO PITCH

OTHER INFO

RATE & FREQUENCY

Client Profile

Client:

MONTH FOCUS

STYLE GUIDE

ASSIGNMENTS DUE

ARTICLE IDEAS TO PITCH

OTHER INFO

RATE & FREQUENCY

Client Profile

Client:

MONTH FOCUS

STYLE GUIDE

ASSIGNMENTS DUE

ARTICLE IDEAS TO PITCH

OTHER INFO

RATE & FREQUENCY

Client Profile

Client:

MONTH FOCUS

STYLE GUIDE

ASSIGNMENTS DUE

ARTICLE IDEAS TO PITCH

OTHER INFO

RATE & FREQUENCY

Pitch
Trackers

MAXIMIZE YOUR FREELANCE EFFORTS BY TRACKING
PITCHES AND RE-PITCHING TO NEW OUTLETS.

Pitch Tracker

IDEA	OUTLET	DATE PITCHED	FOLLOW UP	RESULT	PLAN B

Pitch Tracker

IDEA	OUTLET	DATE PITCHED	FOLLOW UP	RESULT	PLAN B

Pitch Tracker

IDEA	OUTLET	DATE PITCHED	FOLLOW UP	RESULT	PLAN B

Pitch Tracker

IDEA	OUTLET	DATE PITCHED	FOLLOW UP	RESULT	PLAN B

Pitch Tracker

IDEA	OUTLET	DATE PITCHED	FOLLOW UP	RESULT	PLAN B

Pitch Tracker

IDEA	OUTLET	DATE PITCHED	FOLLOW UP	RESULT	PLAN B

Pitch Tracker

IDEA	OUTLET	DATE PITCHED	FOLLOW UP	RESULT	PLAN B

Pitch Tracker

IDEA	OUTLET	DATE PITCHED	FOLLOW UP	RESULT	PLAN B

Pitch Tracker

IDEA	OUTLET	DATE PITCHED	FOLLOW UP	RESULT	PLAN B

Pitch Tracker

IDEA	OUTLET	DATE PITCHED	FOLLOW UP	RESULT	PLAN B

Pitch Tracker

IDEA	OUTLET	DATE PITCHED	FOLLOW UP	RESULT	PLAN B

Pitch Tracker

IDEA	OUTLET	DATE PITCHED	FOLLOW UP	RESULT	PLAN B

Pitch Tracker

IDEA	OUTLET	DATE PITCHED	FOLLOW UP	RESULT	PLAN B

Pitch Tracker

IDEA	OUTLET	DATE PITCHED	FOLLOW UP	RESULT	PLAN B

Pitch Tracker

IDEA	OUTLET	DATE PITCHED	FOLLOW UP	RESULT	PLAN B

Pitch Tracker

IDEA	OUTLET	DATE PITCHED	FOLLOW UP	RESULT	PLAN B

Pitch Tracker

IDEA	OUTLET	DATE PITCHED	FOLLOW UP	RESULT	PLAN B

Pitch Tracker

IDEA	OUTLET	DATE PITCHED	FOLLOW UP	RESULT	PLAN B

Pitch Tracker

IDEA	OUTLET	DATE PITCHED	FOLLOW UP	RESULT	PLAN B

Pitch Tracker

IDEA	OUTLET	DATE PITCHED	FOLLOW UP	RESULT	PLAN B

Invoice
Trackers

STAY ON TOP OF INVOICES AND KEEP TRACK OF HOW
MUCH YOU SPEND AND EARN EACH MONTH.

Invoice Tracker

CLIENT KEY: =_____   =_____   =_____   =_____

=_____   =_____   =_____   =_____

ARTICLE/WORK	PAY	INVOICE DATE	SENT?	PAID?	NOTES

EXPENSES: TOTAL GROSS: TOTAL NET:

Invoice Tracker

CLIENT KEY: =_____ =_____ =_____ =_____

=_____ =_____ =_____ =_____

ARTICLE/WORK	PAY	INVOICE DATE	SENT?	PAID?	NOTES

EXPENSES: TOTAL GROSS: TOTAL NET:

MONTH/YEAR:

Invoice Tracker

CLIENT KEY: =_____   =_____   =_____   =_____

=_____   =_____   =_____   =_____

ARTICLE/WORK	PAY	INVOICE DATE	SENT?	PAID?	NOTES

EXPENSES: TOTAL GROSS: TOTAL NET:

MONTH/YEAR:

Invoice Tracker

CLIENT KEY: =_____   =_____   =_____   =_____

=_____   =_____   =_____   =_____

ARTICLE/WORK	PAY	INVOICE DATE	SENT?	PAID?	NOTES

EXPENSES: TOTAL GROSS: TOTAL NET:

Invoice Tracker

CLIENT KEY: =_____   =_____   =_____   =_____

=_____   =_____   =_____   =_____

ARTICLE/WORK	PAY	INVOICE DATE	SENT?	PAID?	NOTES

EXPENSES: TOTAL GROSS: TOTAL NET:

Invoice Tracker

CLIENT KEY: =_____   =_____   =_____   =_____

=_____   =_____   =_____   =_____

ARTICLE/WORK	PAY	INVOICE DATE	SENT?	PAID?	NOTES

EXPENSES: TOTAL GROSS: TOTAL NET:

Invoice Tracker

CLIENT KEY: =_____   =_____   =_____   =_____

=_____   =_____   =_____   =_____

ARTICLE/WORK	PAY	INVOICE DATE	SENT?	PAID?	NOTES

EXPENSES: TOTAL GROSS: TOTAL NET:

Invoice Tracker

CLIENT KEY: =_____   =_____   =_____   =_____

=_____   =_____   =_____   =_____

ARTICLE/WORK	PAY	INVOICE DATE	SENT?	PAID?	NOTES

EXPENSES: TOTAL GROSS: TOTAL NET:

Invoice Tracker

CLIENT KEY: =_____   =_____   =_____   =_____

=_____   =_____   =_____   =_____

ARTICLE/WORK	PAY	INVOICE DATE	SENT?	PAID?	NOTES

EXPENSES: TOTAL GROSS: TOTAL NET:

Invoice Tracker

CLIENT KEY: =_____ =_____ =_____ =_____

=_____ =_____ =_____ =_____

ARTICLE/WORK	PAY	INVOICE DATE	SENT?	PAID?	NOTES

EXPENSES: TOTAL GROSS: TOTAL NET:

Invoice Tracker

CLIENT KEY: =_____   =_____   =_____   =_____

=_____   =_____   =_____   =_____

ARTICLE/WORK	PAY	INVOICE DATE	SENT?	PAID?	NOTES

EXPENSES: TOTAL GROSS: TOTAL NET:

Invoice Tracker

CLIENT KEY: =_____   =_____   =_____   =_____

=_____   =_____   =_____   =_____

ARTICLE/WORK	PAY	INVOICE DATE	SENT?	PAID?	NOTES

EXPENSES: TOTAL GROSS: TOTAL NET:

Weekly Goals

PLAN OUT YOUR WEEKLY WRITING AND INCOME GOALS.

Weekly Writing Goals

WEEKLY INCOME GOAL:_____ / ___ DAYS WORKING = _____ DAILY INCOME GOAL

MONDAY

- _____
- _____
- _____
- _____

TUESDAY

- _____
- _____
- _____
- _____

WEDNESDAY

- _____
- _____
- _____
- _____

THURSDAY

- _____
- _____
- _____
- _____

FRIDAY

- _____
- _____
- _____
- _____

SATURDAY/SUNDAY

- _____
- _____
- _____
- _____

CLIENT OUTREACH GOALS

DUE THIS WEEK

WORK AHEAD GOALS

INCOME GOAL MET? Y/N

PRODUCTIVITY SCORE:
1 2 3 4 5 6 7 8 9 10

Weekly Writing Goals

WEEKLY INCOME GOAL:_____ / ___ DAYS WORKING = _____ DAILY INCOME GOAL

MONDAY

- _____
- _____
- _____
- _____

TUESDAY

- _____
- _____
- _____
- _____

WEDNESDAY

- _____
- _____
- _____
- _____

THURSDAY

- _____
- _____
- _____
- _____

FRIDAY

- _____
- _____
- _____
- _____

SATURDAY/SUNDAY

- _____
- _____
- _____
- _____

CLIENT OUTREACH GOALS

DUE THIS WEEK

WORK AHEAD GOALS

INCOME GOAL MET? Y/N

PRODUCTIVITY SCORE:
1 2 3 4 5 6 7 8 9 10

Weekly Writing Goals

WEEKLY INCOME GOAL:_____ / ___ DAYS WORKING = _____ DAILY INCOME GOAL

MONDAY

- [ ] _____
- [ ] _____
- [ ] _____
- [ ] _____

TUESDAY

- [ ] _____
- [ ] _____
- [ ] _____
- [ ] _____

WEDNESDAY

- [ ] _____
- [ ] _____
- [ ] _____
- [ ] _____

THURSDAY

- [ ] _____
- [ ] _____
- [ ] _____
- [ ] _____

FRIDAY

- [ ] _____
- [ ] _____
- [ ] _____
- [ ] _____

SATURDAY/SUNDAY

- [ ] _____
- [ ] _____
- [ ] _____
- [ ] _____

CLIENT OUTREACH GOALS

DUE THIS WEEK

WORK AHEAD GOALS

INCOME GOAL MET? Y/N

PRODUCTIVITY SCORE:
1 2 3 4 5 6 7 8 9 10

Weekly Writing Goals

WEEKLY INCOME GOAL:_____ / ___ DAYS WORKING = _____ DAILY INCOME GOAL

MONDAY

- _____
- _____
- _____
- _____

TUESDAY

- _____
- _____
- _____
- _____

WEDNESDAY

- _____
- _____
- _____
- _____

THURSDAY

- _____
- _____
- _____
- _____

FRIDAY

- _____
- _____
- _____
- _____

SATURDAY/SUNDAY

- _____
- _____
- _____
- _____

CLIENT OUTREACH GOALS

DUE THIS WEEK

WORK AHEAD GOALS

INCOME GOAL MET? Y/N

PRODUCTIVITY SCORE:
1 2 3 4 5 6 7 8 9 10

Weekly Writing Goals

WEEKLY INCOME GOAL:_____ / ___ DAYS WORKING = _____ DAILY INCOME GOAL

MONDAY

SATURDAY/SUNDAY

TUESDAY

WEDNESDAY

THURSDAY

FRIDAY

CLIENT OUTREACH GOALS

DUE THIS WEEK

WORK AHEAD GOALS

INCOME GOAL MET? Y/N

PRODUCTIVITY SCORE:
1 2 3 4 5 6 7 8 9 10

Weekly Writing Goals

WEEKLY INCOME GOAL:_____ / ___ DAYS WORKING = _____ DAILY INCOME GOAL

MONDAY

- _____
- _____
- _____
- _____

TUESDAY

- _____
- _____
- _____
- _____

WEDNESDAY

- _____
- _____
- _____
- _____

THURSDAY

- _____
- _____
- _____
- _____

FRIDAY

- _____
- _____
- _____
- _____

SATURDAY/SUNDAY

- _____
- _____
- _____
- _____

CLIENT OUTREACH GOALS

DUE THIS WEEK

WORK AHEAD GOALS

INCOME GOAL MET? Y/N

PRODUCTIVITY SCORE:
1 2 3 4 5 6 7 8 9 10

Weekly Writing Goals

WEEKLY INCOME GOAL:_____ / ___ DAYS WORKING = _____ DAILY INCOME GOAL

MONDAY

- _____
- _____
- _____
- _____

SATURDAY/SUNDAY

- _____
- _____
- _____
- _____

TUESDAY

- _____
- _____
- _____
- _____

WEDNESDAY

- _____
- _____
- _____
- _____

CLIENT OUTREACH GOALS

DUE THIS WEEK

THURSDAY

- _____
- _____
- _____
- _____

WORK AHEAD GOALS

FRIDAY

- _____
- _____
- _____
- _____

INCOME GOAL MET? Y/N

PRODUCTIVITY SCORE:
1 2 3 4 5 6 7 8 9 10

Weekly Writing Goals

WEEKLY INCOME GOAL:_____ / ___ DAYS WORKING = _____ DAILY INCOME GOAL

MONDAY

-
-
-
-

TUESDAY

-
-
-
-

WEDNESDAY

-
-
-
-

THURSDAY

-
-
-
-

FRIDAY

-
-
-
-

SATURDAY/SUNDAY

-
-
-
-

CLIENT OUTREACH GOALS

DUE THIS WEEK

WORK AHEAD GOALS

INCOME GOAL MET? Y/N

PRODUCTIVITY SCORE:
1 2 3 4 5 6 7 8 9 10

Weekly Writing Goals

WEEKLY INCOME GOAL:_____ / ___ DAYS WORKING = _____ DAILY INCOME GOAL

MONDAY

TUESDAY

WEDNESDAY

THURSDAY

FRIDAY

SATURDAY/SUNDAY

CLIENT OUTREACH GOALS

DUE THIS WEEK

WORK AHEAD GOALS

INCOME GOAL MET? Y/N

PRODUCTIVITY SCORE:
1 2 3 4 5 6 7 8 9 10

Weekly Writing Goals

WEEKLY INCOME GOAL:_____ / ___ DAYS WORKING = _____ DAILY INCOME GOAL

MONDAY

SATURDAY/SUNDAY

TUESDAY

CLIENT OUTREACH GOALS

WEDNESDAY

DUE THIS WEEK

THURSDAY

WORK AHEAD GOALS

FRIDAY

INCOME GOAL MET? Y/N

PRODUCTIVITY SCORE:
1 2 3 4 5 6 7 8 9 10

Weekly Writing Goals

WEEKLY INCOME GOAL:_____ / ___ DAYS WORKING = _____ DAILY INCOME GOAL

MONDAY

SATURDAY/SUNDAY

TUESDAY

CLIENT OUTREACH GOALS

WEDNESDAY

DUE THIS WEEK

THURSDAY

WORK AHEAD GOALS

FRIDAY

INCOME GOAL MET? Y/N

PRODUCTIVITY SCORE:
1 2 3 4 5 6 7 8 9 10

Weekly Writing Goals

WEEKLY INCOME GOAL:_____ / ___ DAYS WORKING = _____ DAILY INCOME GOAL

MONDAY

☐ _____
☐ _____
☐ _____
☐ _____

TUESDAY

☐ _____
☐ _____
☐ _____
☐ _____

WEDNESDAY

☐ _____
☐ _____
☐ _____
☐ _____

THURSDAY

☐ _____
☐ _____
☐ _____
☐ _____

FRIDAY

☐ _____
☐ _____
☐ _____
☐ _____

SATURDAY/SUNDAY

☐ _____
☐ _____
☐ _____
☐ _____

CLIENT OUTREACH GOALS

DUE THIS WEEK

WORK AHEAD GOALS

INCOME GOAL MET? Y/N

PRODUCTIVITY SCORE:
1 2 3 4 5 6 7 8 9 10

Weekly Writing Goals

WEEKLY INCOME GOAL:_____ / ___ DAYS WORKING = _____ DAILY INCOME GOAL

MONDAY

☐ _____
☐ _____
☐ _____
☐ _____

SATURDAY/SUNDAY

☐ _____
☐ _____
☐ _____
☐ _____

TUESDAY

☐ _____
☐ _____
☐ _____
☐ _____

CLIENT OUTREACH GOALS

WEDNESDAY

☐ _____
☐ _____
☐ _____
☐ _____

DUE THIS WEEK

THURSDAY

☐ _____
☐ _____
☐ _____
☐ _____

WORK AHEAD GOALS

FRIDAY

☐ _____
☐ _____
☐ _____
☐ _____

INCOME GOAL MET? Y/N

PRODUCTIVITY SCORE:
1 2 3 4 5 6 7 8 9 10

Weekly Writing Goals

WEEKLY INCOME GOAL:_____ / ___ DAYS WORKING = _____ DAILY INCOME GOAL

MONDAY

- ☐ _____
- ☐ _____
- ☐ _____
- ☐ _____

TUESDAY

- ☐ _____
- ☐ _____
- ☐ _____
- ☐ _____

WEDNESDAY

- ☐ _____
- ☐ _____
- ☐ _____
- ☐ _____

THURSDAY

- ☐ _____
- ☐ _____
- ☐ _____
- ☐ _____

FRIDAY

- ☐ _____
- ☐ _____
- ☐ _____
- ☐ _____

SATURDAY/SUNDAY

- ☐ _____
- ☐ _____
- ☐ _____
- ☐ _____

CLIENT OUTREACH GOALS

DUE THIS WEEK

WORK AHEAD GOALS

INCOME GOAL MET? Y/N

PRODUCTIVITY SCORE:
1 2 3 4 5 6 7 8 9 10

Weekly Writing Goals

WEEKLY INCOME GOAL:_____ / ___ DAYS WORKING = _____ DAILY INCOME GOAL

MONDAY

- [ ] _____
- [ ] _____
- [ ] _____
- [ ] _____

TUESDAY

- [ ] _____
- [ ] _____
- [ ] _____
- [ ] _____

WEDNESDAY

- [ ] _____
- [ ] _____
- [ ] _____
- [ ] _____

THURSDAY

- [ ] _____
- [ ] _____
- [ ] _____
- [ ] _____

FRIDAY

- [ ] _____
- [ ] _____
- [ ] _____
- [ ] _____

SATURDAY/SUNDAY

- [ ] _____
- [ ] _____
- [ ] _____
- [ ] _____

CLIENT OUTREACH GOALS

DUE THIS WEEK

WORK AHEAD GOALS

INCOME GOAL MET? Y/N

PRODUCTIVITY SCORE:
1 2 3 4 5 6 7 8 9 10

Weekly Writing Goals

WEEKLY INCOME GOAL:_____ / ___ DAYS WORKING = _____ DAILY INCOME GOAL

MONDAY

- [ ] _____
- [ ] _____
- [ ] _____
- [ ] _____

TUESDAY

- [ ] _____
- [ ] _____
- [ ] _____
- [ ] _____

WEDNESDAY

- [ ] _____
- [ ] _____
- [ ] _____
- [ ] _____

THURSDAY

- [ ] _____
- [ ] _____
- [ ] _____
- [ ] _____

FRIDAY

- [ ] _____
- [ ] _____
- [ ] _____
- [ ] _____

SATURDAY/SUNDAY

- [ ] _____
- [ ] _____
- [ ] _____
- [ ] _____

CLIENT OUTREACH GOALS

DUE THIS WEEK

WORK AHEAD GOALS

INCOME GOAL MET? Y/N

PRODUCTIVITY SCORE:
1 2 3 4 5 6 7 8 9 10

Weekly Writing Goals

WEEKLY INCOME GOAL:_____ / ___ DAYS WORKING = _____ DAILY INCOME GOAL

MONDAY

- _____
- _____
- _____
- _____

TUESDAY

- _____
- _____
- _____
- _____

WEDNESDAY

- _____
- _____
- _____
- _____

THURSDAY

- _____
- _____
- _____
- _____

FRIDAY

- _____
- _____
- _____
- _____

SATURDAY/SUNDAY

- _____
- _____
- _____
- _____

CLIENT OUTREACH GOALS

DUE THIS WEEK

WORK AHEAD GOALS

INCOME GOAL MET? Y/N

PRODUCTIVITY SCORE:
1 2 3 4 5 6 7 8 9 10

Weekly Writing Goals

WEEKLY INCOME GOAL:_____ / ___ DAYS WORKING = _____ DAILY INCOME GOAL

MONDAY

☐ _____
☐ _____
☐ _____
☐ _____

TUESDAY

☐ _____
☐ _____
☐ _____
☐ _____

WEDNESDAY

☐ _____
☐ _____
☐ _____
☐ _____

THURSDAY

☐ _____
☐ _____
☐ _____
☐ _____

FRIDAY

☐ _____
☐ _____
☐ _____
☐ _____

SATURDAY/SUNDAY

☐ _____
☐ _____
☐ _____
☐ _____

CLIENT OUTREACH GOALS

DUE THIS WEEK

WORK AHEAD GOALS

INCOME GOAL MET? Y/N

PRODUCTIVITY SCORE:
1 2 3 4 5 6 7 8 9 10

Weekly Writing Goals

WEEKLY INCOME GOAL:_____ / ___ DAYS WORKING = _____ DAILY INCOME GOAL

MONDAY

☐ _____
☐ _____
☐ _____
☐ _____

TUESDAY

☐ _____
☐ _____
☐ _____
☐ _____

WEDNESDAY

☐ _____
☐ _____
☐ _____
☐ _____

THURSDAY

☐ _____
☐ _____
☐ _____
☐ _____

FRIDAY

☐ _____
☐ _____
☐ _____
☐ _____

SATURDAY/SUNDAY

☐ _____
☐ _____
☐ _____
☐ _____

CLIENT OUTREACH GOALS

DUE THIS WEEK

WORK AHEAD GOALS

INCOME GOAL MET? Y/N

PRODUCTIVITY SCORE:
1 2 3 4 5 6 7 8 9 10

Weekly Writing Goals

WEEKLY INCOME GOAL:_____ / ___ DAYS WORKING = _____ DAILY INCOME GOAL

MONDAY

- _____
- _____
- _____
- _____

TUESDAY

- _____
- _____
- _____
- _____

WEDNESDAY

- _____
- _____
- _____
- _____

THURSDAY

- _____
- _____
- _____
- _____

FRIDAY

- _____
- _____
- _____
- _____

SATURDAY/SUNDAY

- _____
- _____
- _____
- _____

CLIENT OUTREACH GOALS

DUE THIS WEEK

WORK AHEAD GOALS

INCOME GOAL MET? Y/N

PRODUCTIVITY SCORE:
1 2 3 4 5 6 7 8 9 10

Weekly Writing Goals

WEEKLY INCOME GOAL:_____ / ___ DAYS WORKING = _____ DAILY INCOME GOAL

MONDAY

☐ _____
☐ _____
☐ _____
☐ _____

TUESDAY

☐ _____
☐ _____
☐ _____
☐ _____

WEDNESDAY

☐ _____
☐ _____
☐ _____
☐ _____

THURSDAY

☐ _____
☐ _____
☐ _____
☐ _____

FRIDAY

☐ _____
☐ _____
☐ _____
☐ _____

SATURDAY/SUNDAY

☐ _____
☐ _____
☐ _____
☐ _____

CLIENT OUTREACH GOALS

DUE THIS WEEK

WORK AHEAD GOALS

INCOME GOAL MET? Y/N

PRODUCTIVITY SCORE:
1 2 3 4 5 6 7 8 9 10

Weekly Writing Goals

WEEKLY INCOME GOAL:_____ / ___ DAYS WORKING = _____ DAILY INCOME GOAL

MONDAY

☐ _____
☐ _____
☐ _____
☐ _____

TUESDAY

☐ _____
☐ _____
☐ _____
☐ _____

WEDNESDAY

☐ _____
☐ _____
☐ _____
☐ _____

THURSDAY

☐ _____
☐ _____
☐ _____
☐ _____

FRIDAY

☐ _____
☐ _____
☐ _____
☐ _____

SATURDAY/SUNDAY

☐ _____
☐ _____
☐ _____
☐ _____

CLIENT OUTREACH GOALS

DUE THIS WEEK

WORK AHEAD GOALS

INCOME GOAL MET? Y/N

PRODUCTIVITY SCORE:
1 2 3 4 5 6 7 8 9 10

Weekly Writing Goals

WEEKLY INCOME GOAL:_____ / ___ DAYS WORKING = _____ DAILY INCOME GOAL

MONDAY

- [ ] _____
- [ ] _____
- [ ] _____
- [ ] _____

TUESDAY

- [ ] _____
- [ ] _____
- [ ] _____
- [ ] _____

WEDNESDAY

- [ ] _____
- [ ] _____
- [ ] _____
- [ ] _____

THURSDAY

- [ ] _____
- [ ] _____
- [ ] _____
- [ ] _____

FRIDAY

- [ ] _____
- [ ] _____
- [ ] _____
- [ ] _____

SATURDAY/SUNDAY

- [ ] _____
- [ ] _____
- [ ] _____
- [ ] _____

CLIENT OUTREACH GOALS

DUE THIS WEEK

WORK AHEAD GOALS

INCOME GOAL MET? Y/N

PRODUCTIVITY SCORE:
1 2 3 4 5 6 7 8 9 10

Weekly Writing Goals

WEEKLY INCOME GOAL:_____ / ___ DAYS WORKING = _____ DAILY INCOME GOAL

MONDAY

- _____
- _____
- _____
- _____

TUESDAY

- _____
- _____
- _____
- _____

WEDNESDAY

- _____
- _____
- _____
- _____

THURSDAY

- _____
- _____
- _____
- _____

FRIDAY

- _____
- _____
- _____
- _____

SATURDAY/SUNDAY

- _____
- _____
- _____
- _____

CLIENT OUTREACH GOALS

DUE THIS WEEK

WORK AHEAD GOALS

INCOME GOAL MET? Y/N

PRODUCTIVITY SCORE:
1 2 3 4 5 6 7 8 9 10

Weekly Writing Goals

WEEKLY INCOME GOAL:_____ / ___ DAYS WORKING = _____ DAILY INCOME GOAL

MONDAY

- _____
- _____
- _____
- _____

TUESDAY

- _____
- _____
- _____
- _____

WEDNESDAY

- _____
- _____
- _____
- _____

THURSDAY

- _____
- _____
- _____
- _____

FRIDAY

- _____
- _____
- _____
- _____

SATURDAY/SUNDAY

- _____
- _____
- _____
- _____

CLIENT OUTREACH GOALS

DUE THIS WEEK

WORK AHEAD GOALS

INCOME GOAL MET? Y/N

PRODUCTIVITY SCORE:
1 2 3 4 5 6 7 8 9 10

Weekly Writing Goals

WEEKLY INCOME GOAL:_____ / ___ DAYS WORKING = _____ DAILY INCOME GOAL

MONDAY

- _____
- _____
- _____
- _____

TUESDAY

- _____
- _____
- _____
- _____

WEDNESDAY

- _____
- _____
- _____
- _____

THURSDAY

- _____
- _____
- _____
- _____

FRIDAY

- _____
- _____
- _____
- _____

SATURDAY/SUNDAY

- _____
- _____
- _____
- _____

CLIENT OUTREACH GOALS

DUE THIS WEEK

WORK AHEAD GOALS

INCOME GOAL MET? Y/N

PRODUCTIVITY SCORE:
1 2 3 4 5 6 7 8 9 10

Weekly Writing Goals

WEEKLY INCOME GOAL:_____ / ___ DAYS WORKING = _____ DAILY INCOME GOAL

MONDAY

TUESDAY

WEDNESDAY

THURSDAY

FRIDAY

SATURDAY/SUNDAY

CLIENT OUTREACH GOALS

DUE THIS WEEK

WORK AHEAD GOALS

INCOME GOAL MET? Y/N

PRODUCTIVITY SCORE:
1 2 3 4 5 6 7 8 9 10

Weekly Writing Goals

WEEKLY INCOME GOAL:_____ / ___ DAYS WORKING = _____ DAILY INCOME GOAL

MONDAY

- _____
- _____
- _____
- _____

TUESDAY

- _____
- _____
- _____
- _____

WEDNESDAY

- _____
- _____
- _____
- _____

THURSDAY

- _____
- _____
- _____
- _____

FRIDAY

- _____
- _____
- _____
- _____

SATURDAY/SUNDAY

- _____
- _____
- _____
- _____

CLIENT OUTREACH GOALS

DUE THIS WEEK

WORK AHEAD GOALS

INCOME GOAL MET? Y/N

PRODUCTIVITY SCORE:
1 2 3 4 5 6 7 8 9 10

Weekly Writing Goals

WEEKLY INCOME GOAL:_____ / ___ DAYS WORKING = _____ DAILY INCOME GOAL

MONDAY

SATURDAY/SUNDAY

TUESDAY

CLIENT OUTREACH GOALS

WEDNESDAY

DUE THIS WEEK

THURSDAY

WORK AHEAD GOALS

FRIDAY

INCOME GOAL MET? Y/N

PRODUCTIVITY SCORE:
1 2 3 4 5 6 7 8 9 10

Weekly Writing Goals

WEEKLY INCOME GOAL:_____ / ___ DAYS WORKING = _____ DAILY INCOME GOAL

MONDAY

- ☐ _____
- ☐ _____
- ☐ _____
- ☐ _____

TUESDAY

- ☐ _____
- ☐ _____
- ☐ _____
- ☐ _____

WEDNESDAY

- ☐ _____
- ☐ _____
- ☐ _____
- ☐ _____

THURSDAY

- ☐ _____
- ☐ _____
- ☐ _____
- ☐ _____

FRIDAY

- ☐ _____
- ☐ _____
- ☐ _____
- ☐ _____

SATURDAY/SUNDAY

- ☐ _____
- ☐ _____
- ☐ _____
- ☐ _____

CLIENT OUTREACH GOALS

DUE THIS WEEK

WORK AHEAD GOALS

INCOME GOAL MET? Y/N

PRODUCTIVITY SCORE:
1 2 3 4 5 6 7 8 9 10

Weekly Writing Goals

WEEKLY INCOME GOAL:_____ / ___ DAYS WORKING = _____ DAILY INCOME GOAL

MONDAY

- [ ] _____
- [ ] _____
- [ ] _____
- [ ] _____

TUESDAY

- [ ] _____
- [ ] _____
- [ ] _____
- [ ] _____

WEDNESDAY

- [ ] _____
- [ ] _____
- [ ] _____
- [ ] _____

THURSDAY

- [ ] _____
- [ ] _____
- [ ] _____
- [ ] _____

FRIDAY

- [ ] _____
- [ ] _____
- [ ] _____
- [ ] _____

SATURDAY/SUNDAY

- [ ] _____
- [ ] _____
- [ ] _____
- [ ] _____

CLIENT OUTREACH GOALS

DUE THIS WEEK

WORK AHEAD GOALS

INCOME GOAL MET? Y/N

PRODUCTIVITY SCORE:
1 2 3 4 5 6 7 8 9 10

Weekly Writing Goals

WEEKLY INCOME GOAL: _____ / ___ DAYS WORKING = _____ DAILY INCOME GOAL

MONDAY

- _____
- _____
- _____
- _____

TUESDAY

- _____
- _____
- _____
- _____

WEDNESDAY

- _____
- _____
- _____
- _____

THURSDAY

- _____
- _____
- _____
- _____

FRIDAY

- _____
- _____
- _____
- _____

SATURDAY/SUNDAY

- _____
- _____
- _____
- _____

CLIENT OUTREACH GOALS

DUE THIS WEEK

WORK AHEAD GOALS

INCOME GOAL MET? Y/N

PRODUCTIVITY SCORE:
1 2 3 4 5 6 7 8 9 10

Weekly Writing Goals

WEEKLY INCOME GOAL:_____ / ___ DAYS WORKING = _____ DAILY INCOME GOAL

MONDAY

TUESDAY

WEDNESDAY

THURSDAY

FRIDAY

SATURDAY/SUNDAY

CLIENT OUTREACH GOALS

DUE THIS WEEK

WORK AHEAD GOALS

INCOME GOAL MET? Y/N

PRODUCTIVITY SCORE:
1 2 3 4 5 6 7 8 9 10

Weekly Writing Goals

WEEKLY INCOME GOAL:_____ / ___ DAYS WORKING = _____ DAILY INCOME GOAL

MONDAY

- _____
- _____
- _____
- _____

TUESDAY

- _____
- _____
- _____
- _____

WEDNESDAY

- _____
- _____
- _____
- _____

THURSDAY

- _____
- _____
- _____
- _____

FRIDAY

- _____
- _____
- _____
- _____

SATURDAY/SUNDAY

- _____
- _____
- _____
- _____

CLIENT OUTREACH GOALS

DUE THIS WEEK

WORK AHEAD GOALS

INCOME GOAL MET? Y/N

PRODUCTIVITY SCORE:
1 2 3 4 5 6 7 8 9 10

Weekly Writing Goals

WEEKLY INCOME GOAL:_____ / ___ DAYS WORKING = _____ DAILY INCOME GOAL

MONDAY

☐ _____
☐ _____
☐ _____
☐ _____

TUESDAY

☐ _____
☐ _____
☐ _____
☐ _____

WEDNESDAY

☐ _____
☐ _____
☐ _____
☐ _____

THURSDAY

☐ _____
☐ _____
☐ _____
☐ _____

FRIDAY

☐ _____
☐ _____
☐ _____
☐ _____

SATURDAY/SUNDAY

☐ _____
☐ _____
☐ _____
☐ _____

CLIENT OUTREACH GOALS

DUE THIS WEEK

WORK AHEAD GOALS

INCOME GOAL MET? Y/N

PRODUCTIVITY SCORE:
1 2 3 4 5 6 7 8 9 10

Weekly Writing Goals

WEEKLY INCOME GOAL:_____ / ___ DAYS WORKING = _____ DAILY INCOME GOAL

MONDAY

- [ ] _____
- [ ] _____
- [ ] _____
- [ ] _____

TUESDAY

- [ ] _____
- [ ] _____
- [ ] _____
- [ ] _____

WEDNESDAY

- [ ] _____
- [ ] _____
- [ ] _____
- [ ] _____

THURSDAY

- [ ] _____
- [ ] _____
- [ ] _____
- [ ] _____

FRIDAY

- [ ] _____
- [ ] _____
- [ ] _____
- [ ] _____

SATURDAY/SUNDAY

- [ ] _____
- [ ] _____
- [ ] _____
- [ ] _____

CLIENT OUTREACH GOALS

DUE THIS WEEK

WORK AHEAD GOALS

INCOME GOAL MET? Y/N

PRODUCTIVITY SCORE:
1 2 3 4 5 6 7 8 9 10

Weekly Writing Goals

WEEKLY INCOME GOAL:_____ / ___ DAYS WORKING = _____ DAILY INCOME GOAL

MONDAY

- [ ] _____
- [ ] _____
- [ ] _____
- [ ] _____

TUESDAY

- [ ] _____
- [ ] _____
- [ ] _____
- [ ] _____

WEDNESDAY

- [ ] _____
- [ ] _____
- [ ] _____
- [ ] _____

THURSDAY

- [ ] _____
- [ ] _____
- [ ] _____
- [ ] _____

FRIDAY

- [ ] _____
- [ ] _____
- [ ] _____
- [ ] _____

SATURDAY/SUNDAY

- [ ] _____
- [ ] _____
- [ ] _____
- [ ] _____

CLIENT OUTREACH GOALS

DUE THIS WEEK

WORK AHEAD GOALS

INCOME GOAL MET? Y/N

PRODUCTIVITY SCORE:
1 2 3 4 5 6 7 8 9 10

Weekly Writing Goals

WEEKLY INCOME GOAL:_____ / ___ DAYS WORKING = _____ DAILY INCOME GOAL

MONDAY

- _____
- _____
- _____
- _____

TUESDAY

- _____
- _____
- _____
- _____

WEDNESDAY

- _____
- _____
- _____
- _____

THURSDAY

- _____
- _____
- _____
- _____

FRIDAY

- _____
- _____
- _____
- _____

SATURDAY/SUNDAY

- _____
- _____
- _____
- _____

CLIENT OUTREACH GOALS

DUE THIS WEEK

WORK AHEAD GOALS

INCOME GOAL MET? Y/N

PRODUCTIVITY SCORE:
1 2 3 4 5 6 7 8 9 10

Weekly Writing Goals

WEEKLY INCOME GOAL:_____ / ___ DAYS WORKING = _____ DAILY INCOME GOAL

MONDAY

- [ ] _____
- [ ] _____
- [ ] _____
- [ ] _____

TUESDAY

- [ ] _____
- [ ] _____
- [ ] _____
- [ ] _____

WEDNESDAY

- [ ] _____
- [ ] _____
- [ ] _____
- [ ] _____

THURSDAY

- [ ] _____
- [ ] _____
- [ ] _____
- [ ] _____

FRIDAY

- [ ] _____
- [ ] _____
- [ ] _____
- [ ] _____

SATURDAY/SUNDAY

- [ ] _____
- [ ] _____
- [ ] _____
- [ ] _____

CLIENT OUTREACH GOALS

DUE THIS WEEK

WORK AHEAD GOALS

INCOME GOAL MET? Y/N

PRODUCTIVITY SCORE:
1 2 3 4 5 6 7 8 9 10

Weekly Writing Goals

WEEKLY INCOME GOAL:_____ / ___ DAYS WORKING = _____ DAILY INCOME GOAL

MONDAY

- [ ] _____
- [ ] _____
- [ ] _____
- [ ] _____

TUESDAY

- [ ] _____
- [ ] _____
- [ ] _____
- [ ] _____

WEDNESDAY

- [ ] _____
- [ ] _____
- [ ] _____
- [ ] _____

THURSDAY

- [ ] _____
- [ ] _____
- [ ] _____
- [ ] _____

FRIDAY

- [ ] _____
- [ ] _____
- [ ] _____
- [ ] _____

SATURDAY/SUNDAY

- [ ] _____
- [ ] _____
- [ ] _____
- [ ] _____

CLIENT OUTREACH GOALS

DUE THIS WEEK

WORK AHEAD GOALS

INCOME GOAL MET? Y/N

PRODUCTIVITY SCORE:
1 2 3 4 5 6 7 8 9 10

Weekly Writing Goals

WEEKLY INCOME GOAL:_____ / ___ DAYS WORKING = _____ DAILY INCOME GOAL

MONDAY

- [ ] _____
- [ ] _____
- [ ] _____
- [ ] _____

TUESDAY

- [ ] _____
- [ ] _____
- [ ] _____
- [ ] _____

WEDNESDAY

- [ ] _____
- [ ] _____
- [ ] _____
- [ ] _____

THURSDAY

- [ ] _____
- [ ] _____
- [ ] _____
- [ ] _____

FRIDAY

- [ ] _____
- [ ] _____
- [ ] _____
- [ ] _____

SATURDAY/SUNDAY

- [ ] _____
- [ ] _____
- [ ] _____
- [ ] _____

CLIENT OUTREACH GOALS

DUE THIS WEEK

WORK AHEAD GOALS

INCOME GOAL MET? Y/N

PRODUCTIVITY SCORE:
1 2 3 4 5 6 7 8 9 10

Weekly Writing Goals

WEEKLY INCOME GOAL:_____ / ___ DAYS WORKING = _____ DAILY INCOME GOAL

MONDAY

- [ ] _____
- [ ] _____
- [ ] _____
- [ ] _____

TUESDAY

- [ ] _____
- [ ] _____
- [ ] _____
- [ ] _____

WEDNESDAY

- [ ] _____
- [ ] _____
- [ ] _____
- [ ] _____

THURSDAY

- [ ] _____
- [ ] _____
- [ ] _____
- [ ] _____

FRIDAY

- [ ] _____
- [ ] _____
- [ ] _____
- [ ] _____

SATURDAY/SUNDAY

- [ ] _____
- [ ] _____
- [ ] _____
- [ ] _____

CLIENT OUTREACH GOALS

DUE THIS WEEK

WORK AHEAD GOALS

INCOME GOAL MET? Y/N

PRODUCTIVITY SCORE:
1 2 3 4 5 6 7 8 9 10

Weekly Writing Goals

WEEKLY INCOME GOAL:_____ / ___ DAYS WORKING = _____ DAILY INCOME GOAL

MONDAY

TUESDAY

WEDNESDAY

THURSDAY

FRIDAY

SATURDAY/SUNDAY

CLIENT OUTREACH GOALS

DUE THIS WEEK

WORK AHEAD GOALS

INCOME GOAL MET? Y/N

PRODUCTIVITY SCORE:
1 2 3 4 5 6 7 8 9 10

Weekly Writing Goals

WEEKLY INCOME GOAL:_____ / ___ DAYS WORKING = _____ DAILY INCOME GOAL

MONDAY

- [ ] _____
- [ ] _____
- [ ] _____
- [ ] _____

TUESDAY

- [ ] _____
- [ ] _____
- [ ] _____
- [ ] _____

WEDNESDAY

- [ ] _____
- [ ] _____
- [ ] _____
- [ ] _____

THURSDAY

- [ ] _____
- [ ] _____
- [ ] _____
- [ ] _____

FRIDAY

- [ ] _____
- [ ] _____
- [ ] _____
- [ ] _____

SATURDAY/SUNDAY

- [ ] _____
- [ ] _____
- [ ] _____
- [ ] _____

CLIENT OUTREACH GOALS

DUE THIS WEEK

WORK AHEAD GOALS

INCOME GOAL MET? Y/N

PRODUCTIVITY SCORE:
1 2 3 4 5 6 7 8 9 10

Weekly Writing Goals

WEEKLY INCOME GOAL:_____ / ___ DAYS WORKING = _____ DAILY INCOME GOAL

MONDAY

- _____
- _____
- _____
- _____

TUESDAY

- _____
- _____
- _____
- _____

WEDNESDAY

- _____
- _____
- _____
- _____

THURSDAY

- _____
- _____
- _____
- _____

FRIDAY

- _____
- _____
- _____
- _____

SATURDAY/SUNDAY

- _____
- _____
- _____
- _____

CLIENT OUTREACH GOALS

DUE THIS WEEK

WORK AHEAD GOALS

INCOME GOAL MET? Y/N

PRODUCTIVITY SCORE:
1 2 3 4 5 6 7 8 9 10

Weekly Writing Goals

WEEKLY INCOME GOAL:_____ / ___ DAYS WORKING = _____ DAILY INCOME GOAL

MONDAY

- _____
- _____
- _____
- _____

TUESDAY

- _____
- _____
- _____
- _____

WEDNESDAY

- _____
- _____
- _____
- _____

THURSDAY

- _____
- _____
- _____
- _____

FRIDAY

- _____
- _____
- _____
- _____

SATURDAY/SUNDAY

- _____
- _____
- _____
- _____

CLIENT OUTREACH GOALS

DUE THIS WEEK

WORK AHEAD GOALS

INCOME GOAL MET? Y/N

PRODUCTIVITY SCORE:
1 2 3 4 5 6 7 8 9 10

Weekly Writing Goals

WEEKLY INCOME GOAL:_____ / ___ DAYS WORKING = _____ DAILY INCOME GOAL

MONDAY

- _____
- _____
- _____
- _____

TUESDAY

- _____
- _____
- _____
- _____

WEDNESDAY

- _____
- _____
- _____
- _____

THURSDAY

- _____
- _____
- _____
- _____

FRIDAY

- _____
- _____
- _____
- _____

SATURDAY/SUNDAY

- _____
- _____
- _____
- _____

CLIENT OUTREACH GOALS

DUE THIS WEEK

WORK AHEAD GOALS

INCOME GOAL MET? Y/N

PRODUCTIVITY SCORE:
1 2 3 4 5 6 7 8 9 10

Weekly Writing Goals

WEEKLY INCOME GOAL:_____ / ___ DAYS WORKING = _____ DAILY INCOME GOAL

MONDAY

☐ _____
☐ _____
☐ _____
☐ _____

TUESDAY

☐ _____
☐ _____
☐ _____
☐ _____

WEDNESDAY

☐ _____
☐ _____
☐ _____
☐ _____

THURSDAY

☐ _____
☐ _____
☐ _____
☐ _____

FRIDAY

☐ _____
☐ _____
☐ _____
☐ _____

SATURDAY/SUNDAY

☐ _____
☐ _____
☐ _____
☐ _____

CLIENT OUTREACH GOALS

DUE THIS WEEK

WORK AHEAD GOALS

INCOME GOAL MET? Y/N

PRODUCTIVITY SCORE:
1 2 3 4 5 6 7 8 9 10

Weekly Writing Goals

WEEKLY INCOME GOAL:_____ / ___ DAYS WORKING = _____ DAILY INCOME GOAL

MONDAY

-
-
-
-

TUESDAY

-
-
-
-

WEDNESDAY

-
-
-
-

THURSDAY

-
-
-
-

FRIDAY

-
-
-
-

SATURDAY/SUNDAY

-
-
-
-

CLIENT OUTREACH GOALS

DUE THIS WEEK

WORK AHEAD GOALS

INCOME GOAL MET? Y/N

PRODUCTIVITY SCORE:
1 2 3 4 5 6 7 8 9 10

Weekly Writing Goals

WEEKLY INCOME GOAL:_____ / ___ DAYS WORKING = _____ DAILY INCOME GOAL

MONDAY

☐ _____
☐ _____
☐ _____
☐ _____

TUESDAY

☐ _____
☐ _____
☐ _____
☐ _____

WEDNESDAY

☐ _____
☐ _____
☐ _____
☐ _____

THURSDAY

☐ _____
☐ _____
☐ _____
☐ _____

FRIDAY

☐ _____
☐ _____
☐ _____
☐ _____

SATURDAY/SUNDAY

☐ _____
☐ _____
☐ _____
☐ _____

CLIENT OUTREACH GOALS

DUE THIS WEEK

WORK AHEAD GOALS

INCOME GOAL MET? Y/N

PRODUCTIVITY SCORE:
1 2 3 4 5 6 7 8 9 10

Weekly Writing Goals

WEEKLY INCOME GOAL:_____ / ___ DAYS WORKING = _____ DAILY INCOME GOAL

MONDAY

☐ _____
☐ _____
☐ _____
☐ _____

TUESDAY

☐ _____
☐ _____
☐ _____
☐ _____

WEDNESDAY

☐ _____
☐ _____
☐ _____
☐ _____

THURSDAY

☐ _____
☐ _____
☐ _____
☐ _____

FRIDAY

☐ _____
☐ _____
☐ _____
☐ _____

SATURDAY/SUNDAY

☐ _____
☐ _____
☐ _____
☐ _____

CLIENT OUTREACH GOALS

DUE THIS WEEK

WORK AHEAD GOALS

INCOME GOAL MET? Y/N

PRODUCTIVITY SCORE:
1 2 3 4 5 6 7 8 9 10

Weekly Writing Goals

WEEKLY INCOME GOAL:_____ / ___ DAYS WORKING = _____ DAILY INCOME GOAL

MONDAY

SATURDAY/SUNDAY

TUESDAY

CLIENT OUTREACH GOALS

WEDNESDAY

DUE THIS WEEK

THURSDAY

WORK AHEAD GOALS

FRIDAY

INCOME GOAL MET? Y/N

PRODUCTIVITY SCORE:
1 2 3 4 5 6 7 8 9 10

Article Planners

STREAMLINE THE WRITING EXPERIENCE WITH THESE SHEETS.

Article Planner

TITLE:

PUBLICATION:

DUE DATE:

WORD COUNT:

KEYWORD/ TARGET GOALS:

OTHER INFO:

QUICK OUTLINE

Action Checklist

☐ Research/Stats Gathered

☐ Sources Contacted

☐ Outline Created

☐ Article Written

☐ Proofread Draft & Submit

☐ Revisions

☐ Invoice

☐ Social Media Share & Add to Portfolio

Article Planner

TITLE:

PUBLICATION:

DUE DATE:

WORD COUNT:

KEYWORD/ TARGET GOALS:

OTHER INFO:

QUICK OUTLINE

Action Checklist

☐ Research/Stats Gathered

☐ Sources Contacted

☐ Outline Created

☐ Article Written

☐ Proofread Draft & Submit

☐ Revisions

☐ Invoice

☐ Social Media Share & Add to Portfolio

Article Planner

TITLE:

PUBLICATION:

DUE DATE:

WORD COUNT:

KEYWORD/ TARGET GOALS:

OTHER INFO:

QUICK OUTLINE

Action Checklist

☐ Research/Stats Gathered

☐ Sources Contacted

☐ Outline Created

☐ Article Written

☐ Proofread Draft & Submit

☐ Revisions

☐ Invoice

☐ Social Media Share & Add to Portfolio

Article Planner

TITLE:

PUBLICATION:

DUE DATE:

WORD COUNT:

KEYWORD/ TARGET GOALS:

OTHER INFO:

QUICK OUTLINE

Action Checklist

☐ Research/Stats Gathered

☐ Sources Contacted

☐ Outline Created

☐ Article Written

☐ Proofread Draft & Submit

☐ Revisions

☐ Invoice

☐ Social Media Share & Add to Portfolio

Article Planner

TITLE:

PUBLICATION:

DUE DATE:

WORD COUNT:

KEYWORD/ TARGET GOALS:

OTHER INFO:

QUICK OUTLINE

Action Checklist

☐ Research/Stats Gathered

☐ Sources Contacted

☐ Outline Created

☐ Article Written

☐ Proofread Draft & Submit

☐ Revisions

☐ Invoice

☐ Social Media Share & Add to Portfolio

Article Planner

TITLE:

PUBLICATION:

DUE DATE:

WORD COUNT:

KEYWORD/ TARGET GOALS:

OTHER INFO:

QUICK OUTLINE

Action Checklist

☐ Research/Stats Gathered

☐ Sources Contacted

☐ Outline Created

☐ Article Written

☐ Proofread Draft & Submit

☐ Revisions

☐ Invoice

☐ Social Media Share & Add to Portfolio

Article Planner

TITLE:

PUBLICATION:

DUE DATE:

WORD COUNT:

KEYWORD/ TARGET GOALS:

OTHER INFO:

QUICK OUTLINE

Action Checklist

☐ Research/Stats Gathered

☐ Sources Contacted

☐ Outline Created

☐ Article Written

☐ Proofread Draft & Submit

☐ Revisions

☐ Invoice

☐ Social Media Share & Add to Portfolio

Article Planner

TITLE:

PUBLICATION:

DUE DATE:

WORD COUNT:

KEYWORD/ TARGET GOALS:

OTHER INFO:

QUICK OUTLINE

Action Checklist

- ☐ Research/Stats Gathered
- ☐ Sources Contacted
- ☐ Outline Created
- ☐ Article Written
- ☐ Proofread Draft & Submit
- ☐ Revisions
- ☐ Invoice
- ☐ Social Media Share & Add to Portfolio

Article Planner

TITLE:

PUBLICATION:

DUE DATE:

WORD COUNT:

KEYWORD/ TARGET GOALS:

OTHER INFO:

QUICK OUTLINE

Action Checklist

☐ Research/Stats Gathered

☐ Sources Contacted

☐ Outline Created

☐ Article Written

☐ Proofread Draft & Submit

☐ Revisions

☐ Invoice

☐ Social Media Share & Add to Portfolio

Article Planner

TITLE:

PUBLICATION:

DUE DATE:

WORD COUNT:

KEYWORD/ TARGET GOALS:

OTHER INFO:

QUICK OUTLINE

Action Checklist

☐ Research/Stats Gathered

☐ Sources Contacted

☐ Outline Created

☐ Article Written

☐ Proofread Draft & Submit

☐ Revisions

☐ Invoice

☐ Social Media Share & Add to Portfolio

Article Planner

TITLE:

PUBLICATION:

DUE DATE:

WORD COUNT:

KEYWORD/ TARGET GOALS:

OTHER INFO:

QUICK OUTLINE

Action Checklist

☐ Research/Stats Gathered

☐ Sources Contacted

☐ Outline Created

☐ Article Written

☐ Proofread Draft & Submit

☐ Revisions

☐ Invoice

☐ Social Media Share & Add to Portfolio

Article Planner

TITLE:

PUBLICATION:

DUE DATE:

WORD COUNT:

KEYWORD/ TARGET GOALS:

OTHER INFO:

QUICK OUTLINE

Action Checklist

☐ Research/Stats Gathered

☐ Sources Contacted

☐ Outline Created

☐ Article Written

☐ Proofread Draft & Submit

☐ Revisions

☐ Invoice

☐ Social Media Share & Add to Portfolio

Article Planner

TITLE:

PUBLICATION:

DUE DATE:

WORD COUNT:

KEYWORD/ TARGET GOALS:

OTHER INFO:

QUICK OUTLINE

Action Checklist

☐ Research/Stats Gathered

☐ Sources Contacted

☐ Outline Created

☐ Article Written

☐ Proofread Draft & Submit

☐ Revisions

☐ Invoice

☐ Social Media Share & Add to Portfolio

Article Planner

TITLE:

PUBLICATION:

DUE DATE:

WORD COUNT:

KEYWORD/ TARGET GOALS:

OTHER INFO:

QUICK OUTLINE

Action Checklist

- ☐ Research/Stats Gathered
- ☐ Sources Contacted
- ☐ Outline Created
- ☐ Article Written
- ☐ Proofread Draft & Submit
- ☐ Revisions
- ☐ Invoice
- ☐ Social Media Share & Add to Portfolio

Article Planner

TITLE:

PUBLICATION:

DUE DATE:

WORD COUNT:

KEYWORD/ TARGET GOALS:

OTHER INFO:

QUICK OUTLINE

Action Checklist

☐ Research/Stats Gathered

☐ Sources Contacted

☐ Outline Created

☐ Article Written

☐ Proofread Draft & Submit

☐ Revisions

☐ Invoice

☐ Social Media Share & Add to Portfolio

Article Planner

TITLE:

PUBLICATION:

DUE DATE:

WORD COUNT:

KEYWORD/ TARGET GOALS:

OTHER INFO:

QUICK OUTLINE

Action Checklist

☐ Research/Stats Gathered

☐ Sources Contacted

☐ Outline Created

☐ Article Written

☐ Proofread Draft & Submit

☐ Revisions

☐ Invoice

☐ Social Media Share & Add to Portfolio

Article Planner

TITLE:

PUBLICATION:

DUE DATE:

WORD COUNT:

KEYWORD/ TARGET GOALS:

OTHER INFO:

QUICK OUTLINE

Action Checklist

☐ Research/Stats Gathered

☐ Sources Contacted

☐ Outline Created

☐ Article Written

☐ Proofread Draft & Submit

☐ Revisions

☐ Invoice

☐ Social Media Share & Add to Portfolio

Article Planner

TITLE:

PUBLICATION:

DUE DATE:

WORD COUNT:

KEYWORD/ TARGET GOALS:

OTHER INFO:

QUICK
OUTLINE

Action Checklist

☐ Research/Stats Gathered

☐ Sources Contacted

☐ Outline Created

☐ Article Written

☐ Proofread Draft & Submit

☐ Revisions

☐ Invoice

☐ Social Media Share &
Add to Portfolio

Article Planner

TITLE:

PUBLICATION:

DUE DATE:

WORD COUNT:

KEYWORD/ TARGET GOALS:

OTHER INFO:

QUICK OUTLINE

Action Checklist

☐ Research/Stats Gathered

☐ Sources Contacted

☐ Outline Created

☐ Article Written

☐ Proofread Draft & Submit

☐ Revisions

☐ Invoice

☐ Social Media Share & Add to Portfolio

Article Planner

TITLE:

PUBLICATION:

DUE DATE:

WORD COUNT:

KEYWORD/ TARGET GOALS:

OTHER INFO:

QUICK OUTLINE

Action Checklist

- ☐ Research/Stats Gathered
- ☐ Sources Contacted
- ☐ Outline Created
- ☐ Article Written
- ☐ Proofread Draft & Submit
- ☐ Revisions
- ☐ Invoice
- ☐ Social Media Share & Add to Portfolio

Made in the USA
Lexington, KY
20 January 2019